GET OUT ALIVE!

ESCAPE FROM THE BONE EATER

Julie K. Lundgren

Published in the United States of America by Cherry Lake Publishing Group
Ann Arbor, Michigan
www.cherrylakepublishing.com

Reading Adviser: Beth Walker Gambro, MS, Ed., Reading Consultant, Yorkville, IL

Photo Credits:
© Niko Schoefer/Shutterstock, cover, contents page (hyena), © Ward Poppe/Shutterstock cover (meerkats), © fiestachka/Shutterstock (graphic on cover and throughout book); © Cassette Bleue/Shutterstock, speech bubbles throughout; © Nazarkru/Shutterstock, yellow bursts throughout; © Viacheslav Lopatin/Shutterstock (map), Nick Dale Photo/Shutterstock (hyenas) page 4; © Lars Royal/Shutterstock (top), Chedko/Shutterstock page 5; © Miroslav Srb/Shutterstock page 6; © Jandrie Lombard/Shutterstock page 7; © Berengere CAVALIER/Shutterstock Page 8; PlanetWild/Shutterstock (top), MintImages/Shutterstock page 9; © Ondrej Prosicky/Shutterstock page 10; © Henk Bogaard/Shutterstock (top), © Michael Rads/Shutterstock page 11; © Anan Kaewkhammul/Shutterstock page 12; © Kale Nahang/Shutterstock (millipede), © Milan Zygmunt/Shutterstock (scorpion), Tomparsons93/Shutterstock (meerkat) page 13; © EcoPrint/Shutterstock (top), Alfonso Vennari/Shutterstock page 14; © Photography Phor Phun/Shutterstock page 15 and page 19 (both photos); © CAMILO RESTREPO AGUIRRE/Shutterstock page 16; © Craig Russell/Shutterstock (top), Marcel Groen/Shutterstock page 17; © anetapics/Shutterstock page 18; © Melnikov Dmitriy/Shutterstock page 20; © Reto Buehler/Shuttersock (top), © AussieD/Shutterstock page 21; © TOBEphoto/Shutterstock (top), Holly Auchincloss/Shutterstock page 22; © Wirestock Creators/Shutterstock (top), © tawa--mana/Shutterstock,

Produced for Cherry Lake Publishing by bluedooreducation.com

Copyright © 2026 by Cherry Lake Publishing Group

All rights reserved. No part of this book may be reproduced or utilized in any form or by any means without written permission from the publisher.

Library of Congress Cataloging-in-Publication Data has been filed and is available at catalog.loc.gov.

Printed in the United States of America

Note from Publisher: Websites change regularly, and their future contents are outside of our control. Supervise children when conducting any recommended online searches for extended learning opportunities.

About the Author

Julie K. Lundgren grew up in northern Minnesota near Lake Superior. She delighted in picking berries, finding cool rocks, and trekking in the woods. She still does! Julie's interest in nature science led her to a degree in biology. She adores her family, her sweet cat, and Adventure Days.

CONTENTS

A BONE-CRACKING BITE.................. 4

I AM A SUPER PREDATOR! 8

SCORPION KILLER......................... 12

BUILT TO DEFEND! 18

GET OUT ALIVE!.......................... 20

FIND OUT MORE........................... 24

GLOSSARY.................................... 24

INDEX.. 24

A BONE-CRACKING BITE

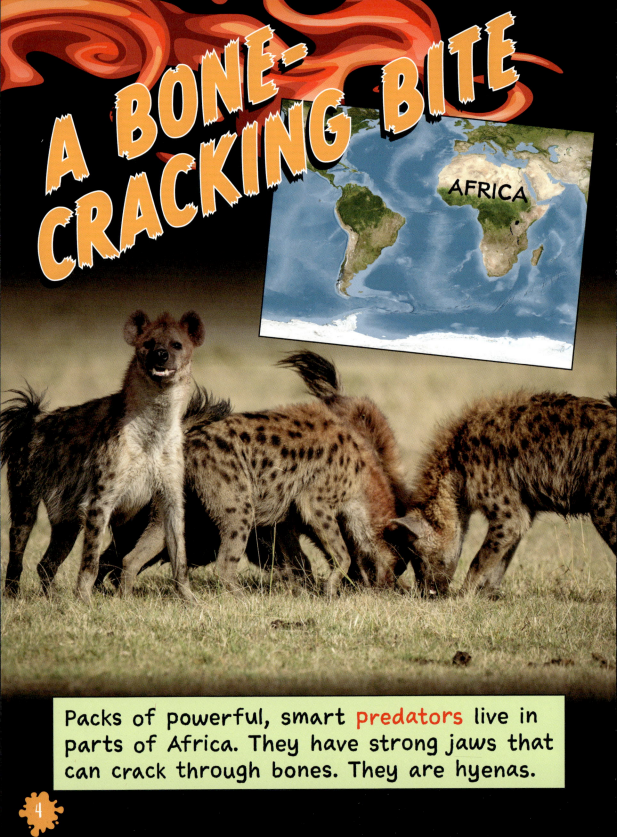

Packs of powerful, smart predators live in parts of Africa. They have strong jaws that can crack through bones. They are hyenas.

With their large hearts and lungs, and long front legs, hyenas easily run long distances looking for food every day.

HYENAS CAN RUN UP TO 37 MILES (59.5 KILOMETERS) PER HOUR WHEN CHASING PREY.

A HYENA'S JAW CAN BITE 7 TIMES STRONGER THAN A HUMAN'S.

HYENAS COMMUNICATE WITH EACH OTHER IN DIFFERENT WAYS. THEY GRUNT, GIGGLE, WHOOP, GROWL, SQUEAL, CACKLE, HOWL, AND GROAN.

HYENAS ONLY FEAR LIONS AND PEOPLE.

Hyenas live in packs of 10 to 100, called clans. Females are bigger than males and lead the clan. Females also lead the hunts and eat first.

We live and hunt together. We protect each other and our young. We survive better together than alone.

AFTER A KILL, HYENAS CAN EAT UP TO 35 POUNDS (ALMOST 16 KILOGRAMS) OF FOOD AT A TIME. IF A LION SHOWS UP, A HYENA CALLS TO ITS CLAN FOR HELP PROTECTING THE KILL AND EACH OTHER.

Hyena mothers and cubs live together in group dens for protection. Adult males live at the edges of the den and take part in hunts.

SCORPION KILLER

Meerkats look sweet and cuddly but they are fierce predators. These small hunters catch and eat insects, centipedes, eggs, snakes, birds, and worms. They will also eat venomous millipedes and scorpions.

MILLIPEDES HAVE A VENOMOUS COATING TO STOP PREDATORS. MEERKATS DRAG MILLIPEDES THROUGH THE SAND TO REMOVE THE COATING BEFORE EATING THEM.

Scorpions defend using their venomous tail stingers. Meerkats rip off the stinger before the scorpion can sting.

Meerkats live in groups called gangs or mobs. Mobs have 30 or 40 meerkats. They live in dens. One mob may move between 2 or 3 den sites.

MEERKATS LIVE IN LARGE UNDERGROUND DENS WITH MANY ENTRIES AND EXITS, AND EVEN A SEPARATE TOILET CHAMBER.

Meerkats leave the den to look for food together. They will dig a **bolt hole** in case of emergency. One or two meerkats watch for danger while the mob **forages**.

We take turns standing guard at the den to watch for predators, including hungry hyenas.

THE GUARD MAKES AN ALARM CALL IF IT SEES DANGER AND THE MOB DIVES FOR THE DEN.

"Under my tail, I have a stinky scent gland for marking my territory. I have sharp teeth and claws."

Researchers are learning the meerkat's language. Its calls, chirps, twills, squeals, and barks can tell other meerkats about a predator from land or sky, how far away it is, and how great the danger is.

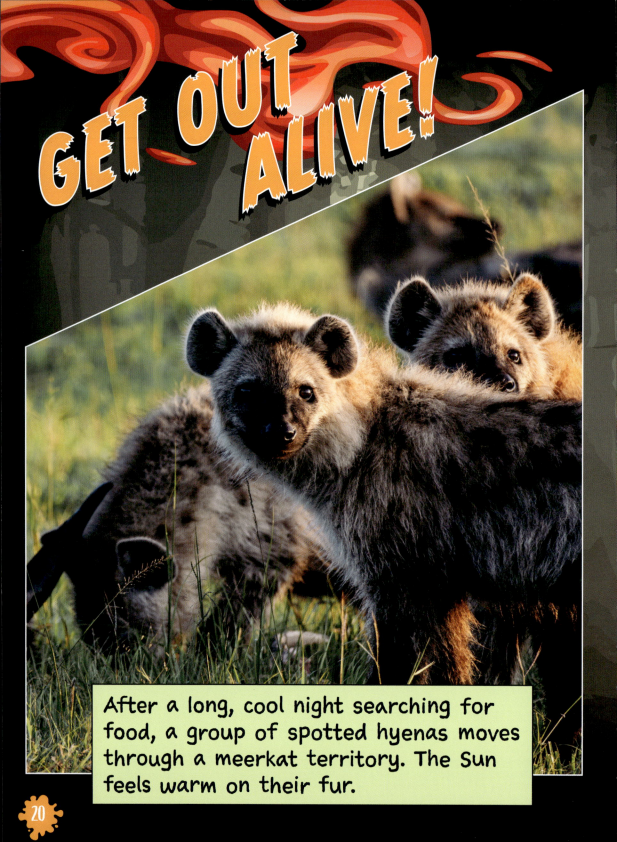

GET OUT ALIVE!

After a long, cool night searching for food, a group of spotted hyenas moves through a meerkat territory. The Sun feels warm on their fur.

The hyena creeps closer. The meerkat guard spots it! Is it too late? Sound the alarm!

The hyena chases one of the meerkats. The meerkat runs, twisting and turning. It kicks up dust and sand into the hyena's eyes. It disappears into the thick dust clouds.

Blinded by the dust, the hyena snaps its jaws where it hears the meerkat. Too late! The meerkat reaches its bolt hole. It scurries down to safety.

Find Out More

Books

Betances, Roberto. *Hyenas Eat Bones*, New York, NY: Gareth Stevens, 2018

Wilson, Rachel M. *Social Lives of Meerkats*, Vero Beach, FL: Rourke Educational Media, 2017

Websites

Search these online sources with an adult:

Hyenas | National Geographic Kids

Meerkats | Britannica

Glossary

bolt hole (BOLT HOLE) a hiding spot in the ground for escaping danger

communicate (kuh-MYOO-nih-kayt) to share information and feelings through language

defend (dih-FEND) to protect from harm

forages (FOR-uh-jiz) searches for food

grooming (GROO-ming) combing and cleaning of an animal's fur

predators (PREH-duh-terz) animals that kill and eat other animals

researchers (REE-surch-urz) people that collect information about something through reading, investigating, or experimenting

scavenge (SKAV-uhnj) to eat the remains of dead animals

territories (TER-ih-tor-eez) large areas of land that animals defend and use

venomous (VEN-uh-muss) containing poison made by the animal itself, used to kill prey or defend itself

Index

bolt hole 16, 23
bones 4, 5
den(s) 11, 15, 16
fight 17
fur 6, 18, 20
guard 16, 21, 22

mob(s) 15, 16, 17, 18
predator(s) 4, 12, 16, 18, 19
prey 5, 7
scavenge 5
scent 19, 21
smart 4